GOSPEL INSIGHTS

Gospel
Insights

BRIAN E BECK

The Methodist Newspaper Co Ltd
London

Copyright © Brian E Beck 1998

First published 1995–1997 as individual studies
in *The Methodist Recorder*

All rights reserved.
No part of this publication may be reproduced,
stored in a retrieval system or transmitted, in any
form or by any means, electronic, mechanical,
photocopying or otherwise, without the
prior permission of the publisher.

ISBN 0 9503603 1 7

Published by The Methodist Newspaper Co Ltd
122–124 Golden Lane, London, EC1Y 0TL.

Designed and produced for the publishers
by Bookprint Creative Services
P.O. Box 827, BN21 3YJ, England.
Printed in Great Britain.

Contents

Introduction	7
The Beatitudes	9
Serving God in Secret	12
The Yoke of the Lord	16
Pastoral Care	19
The Vineyard	23
The Great Commission	27
The Man Carried by Four	31
The Sabbath	34
The Syrophoenician Woman	38
Confessing Jesus	42
Bartimaeus	45
A Question of Authority	49
The Magnificat	53
The Presentation of Jesus	57
Mary and Martha	60
Prayer	64
The Rich Fool	67
The Road to Emmaus	70
The Word	73
The Wedding at Cana	77
The Woman Taken in Adultery	80
Jesus and the Spirit	84
The Vine	87
Thomas	91

Introduction

THESE short studies were first published as a monthly series in the **Methodist Recorder** over a period of two years in 1995–97. The order has now been changed to follow the Gospel text instead of being loosely linked to the Christian year. Otherwise they are reproduced here with only minor modifications.

The selection is entirely personal; these are passages which have excited or challenged me. I have tried in each case to pay close attention to language, content and context, to the social and historical background and to what scholars have to say. Above all I have asked myself, what do these passages, understood in that way, have to say to us today?

Two dangers threaten the Gospel interpreter. One is to ignore the text offered to us in the desire to get behind it to Jesus 'as he really was', what he really said and did. That is an important and interesting exercise but very difficult, and we run the risk of remaking Jesus in our own image. Instead we need to listen to what each Gospel writer is saying about him, for the text of Scripture is more important than our historical reconstructions, and each Gospel offers its own insights.

The other danger is that we let the scholarship divert us. The Gospels are very ancient books, four times older than Shakespeare, and in a foreign language. If he can be hard to understand, why should they be easier? So the temptation is to allow them to become remote, just specimens of an ancient culture. But while we must respect the fact that they are products of a faraway time, it is still possible (as with Shakespeare) to hear what they say. What I have heard of their voice I have tried to share.

The original articles were sometimes used by study groups and I wondered about setting discussion questions. But I decided that they might too narrowly channel readers' thoughts. Let the passages speak to you in whatever way they may. The Gospels can be read over and over again, and in the process you might perhaps return to these brief comments for stimulus; but who tries to answer the same exam questions twice?

So I invite you to look again at these Gospel texts. The tools of modern scholarship are important, but there is one requirement that is indispensable: a serious intention to listen. It is summed up in Charles Wesley's familiar prayer:

Come divine interpreter,
   Bring us eyes thy book to read,
Ears the mystic words to hear,
   Words which did from thee proceed,
Words that endless bliss impart,
Kept in an obedient heart.

1
The Beatitudes
Matthew 5.1–12

IN dealing with Matthew's version of the beatitudes it is important to remember its setting in the Gospel. Matthew underlines the authority of Jesus as the interpreter of God's will by presenting the main body of his teaching in five addresses, of which chapters 5 to 7 are the first, on the analogy of the five books of Moses and other five-fold groupings in the Old Testament. Coming at the beginning of the first of the five sections the beatitudes could hardly be given greater prominence. This above all else is what Jesus commands his disciples and what one day they are to teach others to observe (see 28.20).

There is another aspect to the setting. All the teaching of Jesus in Matthew challenges head-on Pharisaic teaching which represents, not just in the time of Jesus himself but for the later readers of the Gospel, an alternative understanding of the will and character of God which, impressive though it is and powerfully presented, and based (like Jesus' teaching) on the Old Testament, is ultimately mistaken. This is brought out not only in what follows (5.17–20, etc) but in verses 3 to 10, where the recurring 'they shall' is emphatic in the original Greek. These are the ones, the poor in spirit, the meek, the peacemakers etc, who (whatever others may say) will enter God's realm, inhabit the promised land and be granted the privilege of seeing God face to face. Only these can be regarded as blessed by God and held up as admirable. The beatitudes are meant to shock.

We see the character of Matthew's beatitudes more clearly if we compare them with Luke 6.20–26. Matthew's version is not (like Luke's) good news addressed to those in poverty and sorrow who are urged to look up in hope because relief is at hand; it is a *description* of who will inherit the kingdom of heaven: 'blessed are those who . . .' Along with this, the emphasis is on spiritual qualities. 'Blessed are the poor *in spirit*' makes the point at the start. So Jesus' first great sermon to disciples begins with a sketch of what the true disciple should look like. It is not surprising that this passage is the traditional Gospel for All Saints' Day.

In a sense there is nothing new about it. All its sentiments can be found in the Old Testament (look, for example, at Psalm 24.3–4, 37.11, 73.1, 107.9, Isaiah 57.15, 61.1–2). But it asserts a vision of what it means to be a human being as God intended, that religious people, then as now, easily overlook or distort. It calls us back to basics.

But it does not stand alone. Often the thought, and sometimes the language, points us to other parts of Matthew's Gospel. 'Righteousness', for example, what it truly is and how it can be attained, is a central theme of all the Sermon on the Mount, so also is the insistence that such righteousness should be a thing of the heart, deep within us, and not just a matter of outward conformity (see, for example, the rest of chapter 5). 'Gentleness' is a mark of Jesus himself (11.29, 21.5). The call to show mercy comes in 9.13, 12.17, 18.33, 23.23. Like verse 9, 5.45 insists that it is those who promote good relationships, even with enemies, who are most like God, can be called God's children and will inherit his kingdom ('sons of God', the literal meaning of verse 45, implies all this).

In reflecting on this passage note especially two aspects. The virtues upheld here are the virtues of the weak and powerless. It is those who are conscious of their poverty, of the goodness they long for but have not achieved, who are to be pronounced happy. It is the reconcilers and the merciful, not those who win every battle, who are God-like; the gentle, not the macho and aggressive, who are to possess the earth. It is a far cry from the images of our time – the 'lucky' winner of millions, the dynamic 'manager', the 'no surrender', 'no turning' politician. It is a far cry, too, from the more confrontational styles of militant Christianity which stress engagement with the powers that be. That Christians who have access to worldly power (as most in a democratic society to some extent do) should use it to combat evil is not in dispute, but the beatitudes are addressed to the truly powerless, who can expect only persecution and ridicule, with no redress. They pose the fundamental question which no disciple of Jesus can avoid, what quality of person are we and what values do we ultimately affirm?

Secondly, observe the element of promise. While these verses are a character-sketch of the Christian disciple they are of necessity more than that. They point us to the dependability of God. They say, not only that it is desirable to be poor in spirit, to hunger and thirst for a righteousness we know we do not possess, but that God can be depended upon to grant what we seek. They are more than a summons to discipleship; they are pure gospel. '*Blessed* are those who hunger and thirst after righteousness' – why? – '*for they shall be satisfied*'.

2
Serving God in Secret
Matthew 6.1–21

THIS passage can be thought of as an analogy of a sermon in itself, with a text (verse 1), three points (verses 2–18), conclusion (verses 19–21) and a massive digression in the middle (verses 7–15). Matthew takes the opportunity of adding to verse 6 further sayings about prayer, occurring elsewhere in other Gospels, which make a variety of points, all different from the main topic of the passage. If we ignore that digression we can immediately see that the three points, verses 2–4, 5–6, 16–18, have a common structure and theme, which can be set out like this:

> When you give/pray/fast
>   don't be like the hypocrites,
>   because they do it like this . . .
>   so as to be seen by others.
>
> They get what they want in full.
>
> But you, when you give/pray/fast
>   do it secretly.
>
> Your Father sees what is secret
>   and will reward you.

Verse 1 sums it up and ties the passage to what is gone before. Literally it means 'Do not practise your righteousness before people so as to be seen' and the word 'righteousness' is the key word for the whole of Matthew 5 to 7. The disciples of Jesus are to pursue a righteousness which exceeds even that of the scribes and Pharisees (5.20) and chapter 5 has spelled out some of the implications of that. Chapter 6 continues the theme, by referring to the three standard forms of religious duty in Judaism (as in Islam), giving to the poor, prayer and fasting. It shows how being a disciple of Jesus will make a difference in this sphere.

We will miss the point if we fail to recognise the style of Jesus' teaching here. He is fond of using exaggeration (a camel through a needle's eye) and satire (straining out a gnat and swallowing a camel). So here, he pokes fun at what was no doubt a very sensible arrangement (sounding a trumpet so that the poor could gather when there were gifts to be given) and urges the impossible (one hand not knowing what the other is doing). Besides, elsewhere he contradicts what he says here. In 5.14–16 we are to let our good works be seen (but for God's glory, not ours). In 9.15 he says that disciples cannot fast – not while Jesus is with them (as he is to the end of the age, 28.20).

All of that drives us to ask, what is he really saying here? When we think about that it becomes clear that the point is not to urge us to give to the poor, pray or fast, but to ask how we go about it when we do. The real issue is motive.

The word 'hypocrite' literally means 'actor', but we ought not to think that it is only used in the Gospels of those who consciously put up a false front. The main thing about an actor is that we are not seeing the real person (especially as in ancient times they commonly wore masks). Those whom Jesus criticises may have been quite sincere, following established custom in what they did. But Jesus' laser eye sees the real, unexamined motive behind our actions and demands a different way of doing things which will really test what our true motives are. Will we keep up generosity, prayer and self-denial when there is absolutely no chance that anyone other than God will ever know? Can we possibly do a good thing without even talking about it afterwards, content that God knows? That is the test.

Of course it is a test of how seriously we take God, and how seriously we take the life of heaven, for the reward spoken of here is no earthly one – the hypocrites get that, achieving in full just what they subconsciously set out after, the admiration of others. Verses 19 to 21 drive home the point. There are all kinds of valuables, tangible and intangible, on which people set their hearts, perishable goods and wealth that can be stolen, honour and fame which eventually evaporate away. There is a different form of wealth, another kind of reward, which seems by comparison to offer so little, but which is the only one that lasts. The real test of all our good behaviour is what we are doing it for.

That is where the word 'reward' causes us problems. It seems to bring a mercenary touch to what is spiritual, as though we were to serve God only for what we could selfishly get out of it.

But that misses the point of what the reward actually is. It is not some bonus handed out to those who have done well. Those who live, not just for God but for God first and God only, will not be content with any compensation except knowing that God is satisfied and sharing that pleasure with him. That is the reward.

All this sounds very austere and negative. Are we never to take delight in pleasing another person? Are we to regard as sin the pleasure we ourselves feel at an unexpected word of thanks? Of course not. But the best in us easily gets corrupted, so that praise becomes not the delightful gift others add to a thing well done for its own sake, but the very reason why we do the deed and the only thing that gives it worth in our eyes. That is why we need always to watch our motives and strive to make God himself our objective and our reward.

3
The Yoke of the Lord
Matthew 11.25–30

A GOOD way into this passage is to read what comes before and after. Chapter 11 begins with the doubts of John the Baptist. Is Jesus the one they are looking for, or is there someone else? Jesus replies by pointing to the things he is doing, essentially humane and liberating. But then the question turns from 'who is Jesus?' to 'who is John?' People are difficult to please. They complain about both men, like children playing games and not willing to join in either weddings or funerals, because nothing suits them. They are not willing to undertake the radical change of attitude and lifestyle that would free them to recognise the voice of God and respond.

Chapter 12 begins with a series of conflicts between Jesus and the religious authorities. At the heart of these is a clash between two perceptions of what God demands of people. Is it a rigid and meticulous observance of religious and moral requirements or something more gentle, where compassion predominates and people count more than rules? Because the rules are broken the Pharisees set out to destroy Jesus. They regard him as possessed by the devil, even when he heals the sick. For Jesus, however, understanding God's will begins not with the law of Moses and its traditional elaborations, but with human need and the joy and light that floods into a person's life when healing and restoration are brought about. So again we are brought back to the question, who is Jesus, what sort of person is he?

All these issues surround Matthew 11.25–30. The best place to start is probably verses 28 to 30, for there the contrast is explicitly drawn between Jesus' teaching and that of the Jewish authorities. To accept the yoke of the law was a standard expression for taking up seriously the practice of Jewish faith. But Jesus insists that, as expounded by the Pharisees, it is burdensome and destructive (see 23.1–15). What God desires is mercy, not sacrifice (12.7). By contrast, what Jesus offers will bring rest and refreshment. His teaching and his way are not burdensome and his yoke is light.

But it is a yoke nevertheless, not to be underestimated. The yoke, after all, was a device for taming a beast, bringing it under control, giving it direction, harnessing its energies to pull a plough or carry a load. A yoked beast has no freedom to go its own way; it is entirely at the bidding of its owner.

Following Jesus involves surrender, obedience and the devotion of our energies to his cause, not ours. But the yoke is easy; it does not chafe, because it is designed to fit. It is right for us, 'natural', not alien to our nature.

That is a hard thing to say. There are many times when obedience to the way of Jesus seems anything but natural and is certainly not easy. Yet in the longer view we may come to see how the hardship of following him is for our good and, perhaps more important, the wider good of others, and in that light was right for us after all. The yoke was made to fit.

It's all a matter of insight and that is what counts in chapter 11, insight and willingness to change. That insight into the truth of things is a precious gift. In one sense the teaching of Jesus was open to all. The message was well published in synagogue and open-air preaching. But as we have seen, some could only regard it as the voice of the devil. The 'wise and understanding' – the religious teachers of the time – could not recognise it; it was hidden from them. Only the simple, the 'babes' who had learned to trust God as Father, could recognise the authentic message for what it was.

It is easy to misrepresent this contrast between wise and simple. It is not an attack on the use of intelligence although from time to time some people claim it to be, as though any use of knowledge or our critical faculties would be a sin against the Holy Spirit. That is just a recipe for getting away with any sort of nonsense. As someone recently expressed it in my hearing, God did not give us heads just to have haircuts. The use of the mind is one of the ways in which we are to love God.

What makes us open to receive God's gift of insight is not intelligence nor the lack of it, but simplicity of heart, gentleness, openness to others, the qualities Jesus himself shows.

That is why Jesus is the one who opens up for us the nature of God. Verse 27 is difficult enough for a number of reasons, but at the very least it means this: if we are prepared to learn from Jesus, ready to allow all our prior assumptions to be swept away, and if need be make radical changes in our lives, he will lead us into the secret of how things are with God.

4
Pastoral Care
Matthew 18.1–20

IDEALLY we ought to take in the whole of chapter 18, for this is one of the five great passages in Matthew in which Jesus' teaching is gathered together (for the others see chapters 5–7, 10, 13, 24–25). It well illustrates two features of this Gospel which we need to keep in mind.

First, it illustrates the preaching method (not much in favour today) by which apparently unrelated ideas are strung together by catchword (the Letter of James is another example). Look for the recurrent words 'little ones' and 'stumble' (or 'downfall' or 'lose faith', depending on the translation you use – literally 'scandal'). They hold the passage together, although there are also underlying themes.

Secondly, the whole chapter illustrates the truth that Matthew is a Gospel for the Church. Here, for example, unlike its use in Luke 15, the parable of the lost sheep is not about reaching out to the lost outsider who repents but about going after the one in the flock who wanders off – pastoral care rather than evangelism.

The passage begins with a question about greatness in God's kingdom, a question already suggested by Jesus' saying in 11.11. A child is the answer. But the child here is a visual aid. There is no interest in this passage in children as such, but on the child-like qualities believers must possess. In order to enter the kingdom we have to become like a child, 'turning', that is changing course, taking on the character of a child. The child we are to receive (verse 5) and must not offend (verse 6) or despise (verse 10) is such a believer.

All kinds of romantic (and some silly) suggestions have been made about what is being called for here. 'Innocence' for example, is not an option. Once you have lost it, you can't get it back (the basic lesson of Adam and Eve). Nor is this a swipe at intellectuals. Simplicity and empty-headedness are not the same thing. The key is in the question in verse 1 and the verb in verse 4. Childlikeness is the opposite of 'greatness'; it involves humbling oneself. It is a challenge both to intellectuals and to everyone else. It means not despising oneself nor putting on airs of false modesty, but taking on that quality which Jesus possessed (11.29), of putting God and others first.

But, as the passage goes on to show, such people are vulnerable, easily hurt, and the other uniting thread in the passage is the regard we must have for the fellow-believers who belong to our company but are so easily ignored or despised. We are not to destroy their faith (verses 6–7), nor, indeed, let anything, however cherished, destroy our own (verses 8–9). 'Scandal' originally meant a trap and came to mean anything that stood in the way of progress in faith or pulled one off the path.

So what might this mean in practice? Some have used this teaching to try to block every new idea or change in the traditional way of doing things – 'we must not disturb the faithful'. And there is some point in that warning; changes can be forced through and long-cherished assumptions shattered without any thought for the impact on those who have not seen the point of the changes we propose and fear that the faith is being betrayed. But if that warning had been followed to the letter the Reformation would surely not have taken place or slavery fought and overcome, to take but two examples. Taken to its limit it is a recipe for stagnation.

But it lies heavily on all reformers to remember how easily fragile faith can be destroyed, and to care for those who find change hard to take and not merely dismiss them as obstinate or as obstacles to be overridden. And if people do start to lose their faith, the Christian thing is to go out after them, like a shepherd after a sheep.

Similarly, if people do us hurt, we are to take every step possible for reconciliation and, as the second half of the chapter with its great parable shows, when they turn to us for forgiveness we are to forgive, whatever they have done, and no matter how often, not because we happen to be well-disposed to them, but because we ourselves have been forgiven so much more. It is in that context, of trying to decide how to cope with those who disrupt the fellowship, that the presence of the risen Jesus is promised.

There is a very Jewish ring to this chapter, as to much else in Matthew. The discovery of the Dead Sea Scrolls at the end of World War II and since has shown how Jewish religious groups of the period were concerned, as this chapter is, about discipline and good relations between believers. There is a rigour about this Gospel; being a follower of Jesus is surrounded by great expectations (see especially verses 8–9).

But there is also a gentleness. People are frail, and

faith and obedience are easily lost. The real test of a Christian community is how great expectations are maintained and yet the wayward are coaxed back and the awkward forgiven. When it is like that the church reflects its Lord, who lays on us a yoke that is easy and light because he is meek and humble of heart (11.28–30).

But mark you, there is not a word here about all this being the job of the pastors in the church. It is how we must all be, one toward another.

5
The Vineyard
Matthew 21.33–46

CONFLICT with settlers is not a new experience in the Holy Land and absentee landlords are known the world over.

In this parable someone (probably a foreigner) buys a plot of land, spends money on planting a vineyard, with all that is necessary for its protection (a wall to keep out animals and a watchtower against thieves), lets it out to tenant farmers and goes abroad. The rent would be a share of the harvest, payable to his representative each year.

The tenants are rogues; there may be a streak of nationalism too: why pay the produce of God's land to a foreigner? So they beat up the agents who come to collect the rent and eventually murder the son and heir. There is reasoning behind that: ownerless land could legally be claimed by the first comer. They calculate that if the landlord is not already dead, one day he will be, and without an heir the vineyard and its profits will be theirs. They do not reckon that he will return, but he does and they pay the price.

It is a story that fits the social scene in Jesus' time, but as Matthew tells it at this point in his Gospel it positively shouts aloud its message. The clues are all over the place. The description of the planting of the vineyard strongly recalls the opening of Isaiah 5, where the vineyard God plants is the nation of Israel who fail to yield the fruits of righteousness for which he is looking. The agents and their treatment recall the prophets and the only son recalls Jesus himself. He is killed outside the vineyard as Jesus is crucified outside the city. The message is that God will take away from the Jewish people and their leaders the enjoyment of God's kingdom and give it to others, the Christian Church.

So the parable gives theological insight into history. The writer of Matthew's Gospel and his fellow-Christians struggled to understand what had been happening in their time. Jesus had come; the leaders of God's people had tried to destroy him; and the result was that now a new 'nation', the Church, was inheriting all the promises and bringing forth the fruit of faith and goodness that apparently Israel lacked. It was not a crude replacement of Jews by Gentiles; there were Jewish believers as well as Gentile ones. But the official religious leadership of the people of God had turned their back on the Messiah and the centre of gravity had shifted elsewhere.

If Matthew's readers needed confirmation of that interpretation of events, it was to be found in the resurrection of Jesus and Psalm 118 which cast such clear light upon it. The very stone which the builders had discarded was now the chief stone in the building and the Lord alone had done it.

Today, 2,000 years on, we need to handle such thoughts with care. We can see only too painfully from Ireland and elsewhere how easily old memories can be hoarded and poison every attempt at reconciliation. There were many reasons for the split between Christians and the Jewish people long ago, with faults on both sides. There is much to be repented of, especially on the Christian side, but it would be wrong for either side today to view the other through the distorting spectacles of the past.

But if Matthew offers this parable as an interpretation of the past, and if it would be wrong to use it just to gloat over those who did not accept Jesus then, what can it say to us today?

Perhaps the most chilling thing in the whole passage is verse 46. Having heard how the tenants try to eliminate the heir, the Pharisees and chief priests contemplate that very thing and are only deterred for the time being by the dangers involved. They do not recognise themselves in the story or heed its warning.

So where do we fit in? We assume that we are represented in the 'others' to whom the vineyard is handed over. We are the contemporary Church who have inherited the promises made to ancient Israel. But the sting there is that 'the others' are people 'who will pay him the produce in due season'. If that is not happening, then we need to see ourselves not as the honest tenants in the parable but as the dishonest ones, who resist the claims of God upon us and use our spiritual privileges for our own selfish benefit. If that is so, we may lose the blessings of the kingdom, while others enjoy them.

The indictment is first of all against the Church (all the Churches) as such. Selfishness, abuse of power, disobedience in the Church are not new, though it is easier for us to recognise such things as we look back on the past than in our own behaviour today. But although there is more to the Church as an institution than the total behaviour of its individual members, we each play our part, one way or another, in its institutional life and contribute, positively or by neglect, to what the Church does. One way or another we shall each of us individually have to answer to God for what we do – and not only at the last judgement. In this parable, when God the vineyard owner comes and calls the evil tenants to account it is not the end of the world, but just a staging-post in the progress of time, a judgement indeed, but not the last. As the millennium approaches, it would be worth asking, where have we failed as a Church?

6

The Great Commission
Matthew 28.16–20

JUST as Helen's face launched 1,000 ships, so this passage has launched 1,000 missionary societies. It has been the inspiration of preachers and evangelists for centuries. Often, however, we quote it without reading what it says and so miss some of its wealth of content.

This is the disciples' first and only meeting with the risen Jesus in Matthew and it takes place on a mountain in Galilee, a rendezvous full of meaning in itself. Known in Old Testament prophecy as 'Galilee of the gentiles' (that is, the nations – see 4.15) and a cosmopolitan area in Jesus' own day, Galilee is where Jesus' own mission has taken place, suggesting from the beginning the wider mission to come. The mountain is where he first taught the disciples (5.1) and healed the crowds (15.29) and where they saw his glory (17.1). In the Old Testament 'the mountain' is where God reveals himself to Moses and to Elijah and in the beginning of Matthew the high mountain is where the devil tempts Jesus with the prospect of universal power. For the readers of this Gospel the mountain in Galilee is a solemn and portentous place. If this is where we are, something big is going to happen.

Jesus begins with a claim to the universal authority he refused to buy on the devil's terms, but which has now been given him by God. Such is the outcome of the suffering of the cross. We are reminded of the great parables of judgement in chapter 25, and especially verses 31 to 46, in which all the nations are brought before the Son of Man. Authority means not that the risen Christ controls everything that happens, but that at the end of the day his kingdom will come and all will have to answer to him for the way they have lived and especially for their response to the weak and the poor.

So, how to live is the really important question and it lies at the heart of the commission Jesus now gives his disciples. 'Go and make disciples of all nations' means just what it says. A disciple is a learner. No Gospel lays greater stress on Jesus as a teacher than Matthew does. The teaching he records is organised in five great blocks, each with a formal introduction and ending, echoing the formal arrangement in groups of five of various parts of the Old Testament. The disciples are depicted as a group of pupils round a rabbinical teacher and in such circles what was expected was that the disciple should learn the teaching by heart and be able to pass it on to others in turn. That is exactly what we have here. 'Teaching them to observe all that I have commanded you'.

But we miss the point if we think that all that is involved is being able to repeat some teaching parrot-fashion. More important than the words as such is insight into their meaning. Matthew's version of the interpretation of the parable of the sower in 13.10–23 lays great emphasis on understanding. Nor is this merely a matter of head knowledge. Just as the ending of the sermon on the mount at 7.21–27 stresses the importance of obedience, so here the key words are 'observe' and 'commanded'.

All this is very Jewish in flavour. We are reminded of such passages as Deuteronomy 11.8, where learning and observing the teaching is all-important, and in a variety of ways Matthew's is the most 'Jewish' of all the Gospels. It is important to remember this, because teaching is so much more than merely advice on how to live. Just as in the Old Testament, 'law', torah, embraces not only regulation and moral instruction but also, fundamentally, God's revelation about himself, so in Matthew the teaching of Jesus includes as its foundation all that he discloses to us about the nature of God for, as the first chapter made plain, Jesus is 'God with us' (1.23).

So for Matthew becoming a Christian is a matter of going to school or, perhaps better, becoming an apprentice, learning from Jesus' words and example the theory and practice of living in God's way.

The reference to baptism in verse 19 comes as a bit of a surprise, for we have not really been prepared for this thought in the rest of the Gospel, but it underlines two essential aspects of the learning process which is at the heart of Christian mission. The first is the break with the past which all such learning involves. As for John the Baptist, so for Jesus there is no entry into the Kingdom of God without the repentance which baptism involves. The second is the new identity, which marks us out from those who live by other allegiances. In Matthew's day, we suspect, that was a more painful reality than it is for some of us. That is perhaps why Matthew's Gospel is pre-eminently the Gospel of the Church, for the Church, in this Gospel, is the circle of learners where the disciplines of living can be learned and practised, the weak can be looked after and the unfaithful rebuked (see chapter 18).

It is also the circle where the presence of the risen Jesus can be experienced (18.20). So in chapter 28 the last words of the risen Jesus to the disciples, and through them to those for whom Matthew wrote, and through them again to us, give the assurance of his continuing presence. The disciples go to all the nations to enrol them in the school of Jesus, not because he cannot go, but so that he may come with them.

7

The Man Carried by Four
Mark 2.1–12

THERE are many unanswered questions if we try to recreate this scene in our minds. How did the bearers come by ropes to lower the man on his bed? What were the people in the house doing while the hole was being dug above them? Why, above all, did Jesus react by talking not of healing but of forgiveness? The commentaries usually say that a controversy about forgiveness has been inserted into what was once a more straightforward healing story.

It is best to set such teasers aside and take the story as Mark presents it. Since Jesus began his public ministry in 1.14, Mark has been building up a picture of who he is and the impact he has both on the people of Galilee and on the unseen spiritual forces around them, underlining his authority and the quality of newness in what he says and does. With chapter 2 we begin a series of episodes in which Jesus is in conflict with the religious authorities which comes to a climax in a plot to kill him in 3.6. So the context helps us to see that the central thrust of this passage is the authority of Jesus and the extent of his powers and the way these conflict with accepted theological wisdom. We need to keep hold of this as we respond to other aspects of the story.

The first is in verse 5, 'when he saw their faith'. It is often said that this shows that healing does not necessarily depend on the faith of the sufferer. Other people's faith and prayers can be effective. But 'their faith' must include the paralysed man as well as the stretcher bearers. We are surely to assume that he consented to being carried to the house, hauled up the outside staircase and lowered precariously through the roof and shared their sense of urgency. The real point, however, is the urgency. They could have waited till the crowd dispersed, but didn't. Faith in Mark's Gospel frequently has this intensity about it. It does not take no for an answer. The woman with the haemorrhage, Jairus, the Syrophoenician woman, Bartimaeus, all exhibit a faith which refuses to give up.

The bearers' faith is shown by what they do. In the story they say nothing, but Jesus recognises faith. The Church is not always so sensitive. We tend to look for a confession of faith in words and, while that has its proper place, the danger is that we may be blind to the real but inarticulate faith of those who do not profess to be Christians. God does not wait until we can put faith into words before he responds to need.

The argument between Jesus and the scribes concerns forgiveness. They are perfectly right in what they ask. Only two parties can forgive a wrong done: those who have suffered it and God who is injured by all wrongdoing. Bystanders who have not been affected have nothing to forgive and no right to declare it forgiven. Where the scribes are adrift is in assuming that no one can therefore ever be assured they are forgiven. The issue is that Jesus has authority to give such assurance on God's behalf. He knows God's mind.

Why forgiveness rather than healing? It was a widespread belief that suffering was a punishment for sin and it would be assumed that this man had deserved his paralysis. Only when forgiveness has been assured, therefore, could permanent healing follow.

That is not to say that Jesus endorsed this view. Other passages in the Gospels rule out such a connection (Luke 13.1–5), if only because all are sinners, while suffering is randomly distributed (see also John 9.3). Mark does not endorse the theory either. Only here in his Gospel does he make the connection. The point he is making is the scope of Jesus' authority. The scribes assume in verse 7 that in claiming to declare forgiveness Jesus is taking the easier option, healing being the harder. How can he prove such a claim? Jesus meets them head-on in verse 9. Yet Mark clearly intends us to see that to forgive in the name of God is the harder and greater thing. Jesus has authority for both.

What hope does this passage hold out that those who suffer may be healed by faith? That God responds to faith cannot be denied; there are too many examples in the Bible and since. But there are also too many examples where people have found healing when they did not expect it to happen for us to say that God withholds healing where faith is weak or absent (compare also Mark 9.24). Anyway, to be forgiven is the greater gift.

We need to hold on to the central thrust of our passage. It is not a treatise on how to get better when we are ill and it does not answer such questions. It is a powerful statement of the fact that Jesus knows the mind of God; that he shows us God forgives sins; and that if you have the courage of faith, however inarticulate, and refuse to give up, anything may happen.

8

The Sabbath
Mark 2.23–28

COMMENTARIES on the parable of the sower regularly point out that the sower walks along the public footpath which lies across his land, scattering the seed far and near. So when, as in this passage, Jesus and the disciples walk along the path at harvest time there are grains within reach to be plucked, rubbed free and eaten.

But it is the sabbath and the disciples were breaking the law – not just human law, but divine law, at least as the religious authorities interpreted it.

The critics are close by and take their objection to Jesus, who as the man in charge ought to take more responsibility for his group (schoolteachers on outings know the problem). The likelihood, anyway, is that the disciples had learned such freedom from Jesus, who was notorious for breaking the rules. At all events Mark gives us here a reply which has stood the Church in good stead in controversy ever since; indeed we can be sure that is why he preserved it.

It comes in three parts, verses 24–26, verse 27 and verse 28.

Verses 24–26 do not answer the precise objection. In I Samuel 21.1–6 David obtains some sacred bread for himself and his company from Ahimelech the priest at Nob (Mark for some reason names him Abiathar). But it was not a sabbath; so there is no strict precedent for what the disciples have done. But there is a principle implied. When hunger is at stake, religious rules can be set aside.

The Bread of the Presence ('shewbread') was put out every week as a sign of Israel's covenant with God. It was an offering to God, not for common use. Only the priests (as with other holy food) were allowed to eat it, when it was cleared away to make room for a fresh baking. So David and his company eat what belongs to God. But in extremes that is justified. The creator who provides for his creatures is not going to put his own dignity before human need or doubt Israel's loyalty if for a day or two the customary symbolic proof of it is missing.

Verse 27 comes nearer to the point. The last day of the week was set apart as the sabbath in memory of God's work in creation. Men and women, slave and free, were to spend a day appreciating the rest God enjoys from his labours (see Exod 20.8–11, Deut 5.12–15). But it was set up for their benefit, not God's, and for their benefit it can be broken. Other needs must sometimes take precedence. For such a reason Jesus will heal on the sabbath and for such a reason the disciples can pluck a few ears of corn to satisfy hunger.

Verse 28 is so general it seems out of place. It seems to say that Jesus has the last word about everything and can do what he likes. But Jesus has based the previous two arguments on the principles already underlying Scripture, not on his own say-so. Logic would suggest that, if verse 28 is true, verses 25 to 27 are unnecessary.

But two small words in verse 28 need to be given their

full weight, 'so' at the beginning and 'even' or 'also' before 'the sabbath'. We see the authority of Jesus in what he has just said. There is no area of life, not even the sabbath, which lies outside that authority. But it is not arbitrary; it is rooted in divine principles implicit in Scripture. At the same time it is demonstrated by his insight in bringing those principles to light.

The history of the Christian sabbath is an interesting one. It begins with Christians in New Testament times and immediately after (those who were gentiles at least) turning away from the seventh day and keeping the first day of the week as the Lord's Day to celebrate his resurrection (I Cor 16.2, Col 2.16, Rev 1.10). It was a day of worship, though not free from work, as in the gentile world there was no such freedom. Then, by the time of the Emperor Constantine, the Lord's Day begins to be officially recognised by the state and laws begin to be introduced prohibiting work.

So the 'sabbatarian' view of Sunday begins, applying to it many if not all of the Old Testament regulations. Sometimes the emphasis is on worship and rest; sometimes it is more negative, on what must not be done. Always, however, it has depended on a state willing to provide for, or even enforce, such a day. In many parts of the world where Christianity is not the dominant faith that has never been the case.

Today in Britain public observance of Sunday is changing dramatically. Whatever our view of that development, there will be few who will remain unaffected by it, and the Church itself will have to consider how best to mark its significance in future.

It will be tempting to fall back on this passage to justify dismissing all scruples about how Sunday is used. 'It was made for us and not we for it.' But that is just where verse 28 comes in. It does not give the disciples of Jesus unlimited freedom to do as they like. Jesus does not abolish the sabbath but assert his authority over how it is used. Above all else disciples acknowledge Jesus as Lord. So the proper response to changing social conditions is not, 'I can now do as I like', but 'Lord, what would you have me to do?'

9

The Syrophoenician Woman
Mark 7.24–30

THIS is one of the passages in the Gospels which make us aware of the muslin veil that hangs between the Gospel text and the Jesus of whom it speaks. There are dozens of questions about what really happened, and yet more about what was going on in Jesus' mind, which the Gospels do not answer. Though they point to Jesus they do not allow us to see him as clearly as we would wish. We have to content ourselves by looking at what they want us to see.

There is no doubt that Mark is describing a supernatural act of healing. Verse 29 cannot mean just that by telepathy Jesus knew the child had got better. There is a chain of events. Because of what the mother says, Jesus speaks; because he speaks, the child is healed.

Why does Jesus not heal her outright? We shall never know. Some commentators have speculated that Jesus was trying to make up his mind about the next move in his mission. Should he turn to the gentiles? On that view the woman's answer helped him make up his mind – except that after meeting her request he turns back to the Jews again, as though it had made no difference.

It is better to follow Mark's lead and listen to what he is using this story to tell us. Remember he is writing for gentile Christians not very familiar with Jewish ways (he has to explain them at the beginning of this chapter). No doubt Jewish neighbours have made them feel inferior and second-class. In such a context the concentration of Jesus on his mission to Jewish people must have been an embarrassment; if gentiles truly have a rightful place in the Church, why did Jesus not go to gentile lands?

Chapter 7 begins with a discussion about uncleanness. It is difficult for a modern western Christian to appreciate how important the notion of contamination was (and still is in many cultures). So it is difficult, too, for us to appreciate how radically Jesus broke with tradition. For the issue about washing before meals is not about hygiene (other people washed too) but about religious purity. For a person to eat with unwashed hands made them unclean in the sight of God. The radical point Jesus makes is that such external contamination has no effect. What matters is the heart, its thoughts and intentions and the behaviour that emerges from it.

So we come to our passage. Jesus is in the region of Tyre, historically one of the great enemies of Israel. So he is outside the Jewish homeland in gentile country. Even there people flock to him though he does not seek publicity. The woman who comes is a Phoenician and a Greek, that is she speaks Greek and is an example of Greek culture and religion. So on two counts she is unclean – as a 'pagan' she does not observe any of the Jewish laws of purity, she will not wash before meals nor eat only kosher food and, more particularly, as a woman she will not have undertaken the required monthly purification. Compounding it all, her daughter suffers from an unclean and therefore defiling spirit.

So Jesus' reaction to her illustrates his attitude to these deep religious barriers between Jew and gentile.

His first response is to state what must have been the underlying policy of his entire mission. Israel is the people God has chosen; the gentiles' time will come, but not yet. The children must be fed and it would be wrong in any household to starve the children to feed the pets ('dogs' was a common reference at the time to gentiles).

But she takes up his analogy. In every household the dogs lick up the crumbs that fall from the table. No child is deprived by that. In the goodness of God there must be something left over which could come to her. So Jesus responds and her child is made well resting quietly on her bed.

So what are we to take from this story? Some reassurance for a start, that the great gentile mission, of which not only Mark's readers but you and I are the fruit, is true to Jesus even though he did not himself go on mission beyond his homeland.

Then surely some lessons from the woman herself: first, that faith does not easily take no for an answer (even though that is sometimes the answer God gives). Faith will test it out and try to see whether what we are asking may not after all be within the purposes of God.

Secondly, she comes as a petitioner. She accepts the classic divide, as Jesus does, between Jew and gentile. There is no trumpeting of 'gentile rights' here, but a simple statement of need and a plea for help. All prayer is request, not demand.

Thirdly, and perhaps most important of all, is the point the whole story in its context makes: it is not who you are or where you come from or what ethnic group you belong to that counts, nor whether you have conformed to all the social and religious conventions, however good they might be, but whether you have a need and are prepared to believe that Jesus can make a difference to you or someone you care about. If that is the case, prayer can get answered. And that has consequences for who is acceptable in church.

10
Confessing Jesus
Mark 8.27–9.1

THERE is a starkness and missionary zeal about Mark's version of this passage. Not for him the daily cross of which Luke's version speaks (Luke 9.23), which can so easily be watered down to the sort of minor inconveniences all Christians have to face if they are to be good disciples. This passage is about the risk of losing one's life.

Nor does Mark simply speak about loyalty to Jesus and his teaching (verse 38), but about losing one's life for the Gospel (verse 35), that is, in the cause of preaching it. Mark takes it for granted that to follow Jesus involves sharing in the work of spreading the good news of the Kingdom of God and *for that reason* taking up the cross. Self-denial is imposed upon us not just because we are Christians but because we are missionaries. We cannot be the first, he implies, without also being the second.

So the setting of verse 38 is the courtroom, the interrogation centre, wherever the disciple is back to the wall, tempted to be 'ashamed' of Jesus and his teaching, that is, simply to disown him. The price will be that we are disowned in turn.

In fact, price and compensation are the key to the

whole passage, the twin foci around which it forms an ellipse. The passage comes midway in the Gospel of Mark. Up until now the emphasis has been on the dynamic power of Jesus in deed and word, with people asking, who is this? From now on we know who he is, but the answer is just as mysterious as the problem. We now know that this mighty one is the Messiah, the anointed agent of God's rule, but we also know that he is going to *die*, not by accident, but because he must (verse 31). That too is part of God's scheme of things, the price of the kingdom.

In the first bit of the passage (verses 27–30) Jesus extracts from the disciples (Peter at least) a leap of faith, 'you are the Messiah', but immediately he stifles it. True as it is, it only makes sense when you also know, and accept, that he will come into the privileges of messiahship by being rejected. Only because of that will the Son of Man come in glory (verse 38) or bystanders see the Kingdom of God come with power (9.1).

So the second section (verses 31 to 33) gives the first its meaning. Peter rebels, but that is because he is in the wrong camp. He cannot see things God's way. If his confession in verse 29 is a great leap of faith, his intervention here shows he still needs to be converted.

Because, as the third and final section makes clear, what is true for Jesus is inescapably true for the disciple also. The price of discipleship is losing oneself; more specifically, losing one's life. There is no escaping that. We may back off, hugging all our precious things to ourselves so as not to lose them, but in the end we shall lose our very selves.

There is no trade-off for this. In the Old Testament there are various ways in which a person can escape the sacrifice of human life. A first-born child can (in fact must) be redeemed by a sanctified swap, the sacrifice of a lamb or a pair of pigeons or turtle-doves instead (Exod 13.11–15, Lev 12.6–8). But not here. If we possessed the whole world we could not swap it for our survival, if in the gaining of it we have lost ourselves already. The only way to real life is by the losing of life.

But there is a compensation. As for Jesus, so for the disciple. Beyond the cross is the resurrection. Beyond dying for the good news of the kingdom is the promise that we shall see the kingdom come. This is not a negative, all-the-world-is-bad, turn-your-back-on-it-all message, but an invitation to set out on the painful path to glory. Who says the price is too high?

We are left wondering whether this passage is really for us. Martyrdom for the Gospel is not the risk likely to be uppermost in most local preachers' minds as they set off on Sunday morning. A traffic accident more likely. Perhaps that is why other Gospels, Luke especially, modify its tone, to make it fit more snugly to everyday experience. But although Mark stresses all this in the starkest terms, there is a price to pay even for those of us who move in gentler circles and never find ourselves with our backs to the wall for spreading the Gospel. And just occasionally, even in our world, it is the ultimate price.

Verse 38, though, is especially forbidding. Disown him and he will disown us. Knowing the pressures we can come under, what if we fail, as surely many do? Is all hope then lost? We do well to take it with the utmost seriousness. But the central figure in the passage with Jesus is Peter and what we remember most about him is that with his back to the wall in the high priest's house he was ashamed of Jesus. 'I do not know him.' Yet after that denial he was forgiven and restored.

11
Bartimaeus
Mark 10.46–52

I SOMETIMES look round a committee room and count the number of people wearing spectacles (usually the majority). For some of us they are little more than an aid to reading, but others would not be able to get about without them and in biblical times they would have been regarded as blind, even if they could see light and some shapes. We may think of Bartimaeus as one such for he could make his way unaided to Jesus, but could not see well enough to work for a living and so was driven to beg.

That is as far as we can go, however, in identifying what was wrong with him. Diagnosing eye disorders is a highly technical matter and in this story we do not have enough clues even to start. Which makes arguments about whether his cure could have a 'natural' explanation a bit futile. For Mark it was a mighty work of the Son of God and not 'natural' at all.

So what are we to make of this story? If you are one of those who think the Gospel stories are there just because they happened (like Auntie Florrie faithfully recording all the events of the day in her diary), then you add it to your store of wonderful things that happened long ago. Or, alternatively, you find you can't bring yourself to believe people could regain their sight just like that and it becomes yet another in a list of unbelievable biblical miracles. Either way, you are not much better off.

But what if Mark had another reason for telling it? What if he wanted his readers to identify themselves with Bartimaeus in some way and learn something about Jesus for their own lives? In that case we can pigeon-hole the problem about miracle so that it doesn't get in the way of our getting the message. Approached that way, the story yields some interesting lines of thought.

One is the contrast between Jesus and the crowd. The bystanders' reaction to Bartimaeus' clamour is typical: 'Shut up, you are causing a disturbance and distracting us from concentrating on this important moment!' Jesus' response is equally typical, 'Let him come.' Suddenly the crowd are all smiles too, 'Cheer up, he's calling you!' That ready response of Jesus, contrasted with the indifference of others, is an important feature in the story.

Secondly, observe the tenacity of Bartimaeus. He will not be put off. He has fixed his mind on the fact that Jesus is Son of David (Messiah, therefore) and can give him sight. This is his one chance in a lifetime. He is not going to let it pass. Jesus later calls it faith: that quality which seizes on a possibility and will not let go, no matter how great the discouragement, and no matter how unlikely others think the possibility is.

But, to keep that in perspective, notice another thing. The last time Jesus asked the question in verse 51, 'What do you want me to do for you?' was at 10.36, when James and John asked the impossible and were flatly refused. Believing the impossible involves risk. Not every impossible thing is granted and there is an insight to be acquired of knowing what to ask for.

Why did Bartimaeus want his sight so badly? It seems a silly question; who wouldn't? With it he could take a full part in society and, above all, he could work and earn a living. But what does he actually do? Although Jesus says 'Go on your way', he follows Jesus. That says volumes about his real priorities and his reason for asking. Jesus as Messiah and leader was more important to him than just seeing. No wonder Jesus could say his faith had saved him.

So when Mark portrays Bartimaeus asking 'I want to see', the request has a double meaning. Physically his optic faculties are restored. Inwardly a new world has opened up. That is why we can make his request our own and take encouragement from the way Jesus responds.

Two more things to notice about this story: first, its setting. It follows immediately after 10.41–45 where Jesus, unlike 'normal' rulers, is shown as the servant of all, ready to give his life as a ransom. It comes immediately before the entry into Jerusalem where the reign of David is welcomed as Jesus rides in on an ass. Only in the Bartimaeus story is Jesus addressed in Mark as Son of David, making explicit the link with what follows. Bartimaeus (and anyone with similar faith) is one of the many the king comes to serve.

Secondly, Bartimaeus follows Jesus on the road. In other words, he becomes a disciple. But we know from 10.32–34 and 38–40, and other passages earlier, where that road will lead, both for Jesus and those who travel with him. We lose sight of Bartimaeus after this episode in the Gospel story, but those who would learn from his story must take the hint. Determined faith leads to the gift of sight and sight to discipleship; and discipleship leads to the cross – and eventually, but not so quickly as to rob the cross of its pain, to Easter day.

12
A Question of Authority
Mark 11.27–33

A LOT of politicians would give their eye teeth to be as nimble-footed as Jesus in this passage when faced with an awkward question.

The questioners are hostile. Chief priests, scribes and elders are the ruling classes of Israel. Earlier, in verse 18, Mark has presented them as set on killing Jesus, afraid of him because of his popular following. So their question is a booby-trap. If Jesus claims authority from God, they will stick a charge of blasphemy on him or shop him to the Romans as a revolutionary. If he makes no such claim, he will be discredited. These are not earnest seekers after truth. Whatever he says, their minds are made up. They think he is dangerous and evil and must be put down.

Jesus counters with a question of his own. What about John the Baptist? Now they are stuck. If they deny he was sent by God, they will lose standing with the people and risk trouble. If they echo what the people say, that John was sent from God, Jesus will accuse them for not acting on it and submitting themselves for baptism in repentance. So they duck the question and give Jesus his escape. 'Neither will I tell you by what authority I do these things.'

Clever; but there is much more to this than skilful footwork. The question of Jesus' authority is one of the central themes of Mark's Gospel. When he begins teaching, people wonder at his authority (1.22); they wonder too at his authority over evil spirits (1.27) and over the wind and waves (4.41). The scribes argue over his authority to forgive sins (2.10) and in one important passage they get it dramatically wrong, ascribing his power over the demons to the prince of demons rather than to God. That is blasphemy against the Holy Spirit, unforgivable, because obstinate, blindness (3.22–30). But the people acclaim him (too enthusiastically sometimes) as, without question, the one from God, who acts in God's name.

So Mark's Gospel as a whole presents a picture of Jesus as a disturber. One who says and does new and dramatic things and leaves us asking 'who is this?' And the answer people give to that question depends on where they stand. For some, the sick, the disturbed, the forgotten, the ashamed, he is the best news imaginable, for he brings release, dignity and hope. They experience his authority and have no doubt about its source. For others, the religious authorities especially, he is a dangerous deceiver because he contradicts so many of the established assumptions about who God is and what God requires.

That helps us to see the real reason why Jesus refuses to answer the question about his authority. If you cannot see for yourself what the answer is from the evidence before your eyes, Jesus making a claim for himself will add nothing. Indeed it might even make things worse. For those who have not made up their mind, perhaps not even begun to be challenged by his words and deeds, labelling him 'Messiah' or 'Son of

God' may encourage them to dodge the question, pigeon-hole him as one more conundrum solved. We all put difficult questions to one side if we think someone else has solved them and we don't need to bother our minds. Jesus refuses to answer the question whether God is at work in him or not because it is we, not he, who must give the answer.

When I think about this passage today I am struck by three things. One is that the question of religious truth is no easier now than it was then. Quite apart from other faiths, there are lots of Christian variants on offer, some more bizarre than others. Unless God habitually contradicts himself they can't all be right. How do we choose? Not just by the labels they wear, for they all make the same claim to truth. In the end we must decide where God's authority lies.

Secondly, the choice faces us in a variety of disguises. To illustrate from the recent past, many will have had to face it over attitudes to apartheid. Did being a Christian really mean, as some claimed, bank boycotts, selective buying of fruit and picketing South Africa House in the rain? Or, as others argued, did the Christian way point elsewhere, keeping connections, using influence and so on? Which voice spoke with the authority of God? It wasn't easy and there was no one to label the answers. People had to choose. There are plenty of up-to-date examples, if you think about it.

But thirdly, these questions are never just theoretical. Keeping to the apartheid example, it was a matter of where we spent our money, how we used our time, whom we sided with in public and (of course, if we lived in South Africa) whether we were willing to go to prison. It is never a matter simply of putting a label on a point of view, but of lining up our whole being behind it.

Jesus continues to be the disturber. He challenges us to recognise him in the dilemmas of the day. But those who say yes to him never need to ask, who gave you such authority? They know.

13
The Magnificat
Luke 1.46–55

THE experts argue among themselves whether these verses really fit in this place. Are they truly a memory of what Mary said, did Luke compose them himself to represent what she might have said or were they originally a Jewish-Christian hymn that he introduced here because it fitted the context? The basic problem is that some of these lines are too general to fit Mary's situation while others are too particular to fit anywhere else. It is that general quality, on the other hand, which has made it possible for the Church over the centuries to use these verses as one of its own hymns. So let us leave aside the problem of sources and think about the passage as it comes in Luke and as we from time to time use it in church.

It occurs at a key point in the narrative of chapters 1 and 2. The forthcoming birth of John the Baptist, the forerunner of Jesus, has been announced; so has the birth of Jesus himself. Both are the result of the intervention of God, not just of human initiative. Now the two mothers meet (verses 39–45). Even in the womb John recognises the presence of 'one greater' (compare 3.16). Elizabeth acknowledges Mary, her cousin, as the mother of her Lord and praises her faith. Mary's song celebrates what has happened, the grace of God to her and the wonder of his saving power for all Israel.

The language of the hymn is very Jewish and echoes many Old Testament passages but especially Hannah's song of praise in I Samuel 2.1–10. In both places women give thanks not just for their child but because his birth marks a significant turning-point in the story of God's dealings with the people of Israel.

It may seem a limitation that the blessings are for Israel (verses 54–55). But Simeon's song in 2.32 will speak also of a light for the gentiles and the rest of Luke's Gospel and Acts will tell how the promises made to Israel come to be offered to all people as a result of the coming of Jesus. There can be good news for gentiles only because God is faithful to his promises to Israel (more of that in a moment).

That Luke sets out Mary's hymn in full is significant. He *could* have written 'and Mary was very happy and gave thanks to God' (how banal!), but by setting out in full the four great canticles of chapters 1 and 2 (Magnificat, Benedictus, Gloria in Excelsis and Nunc Dimittis) he achieves two results. He draws us in to the praise he describes and enables us to share it; still more he creates a 'classic' atmosphere for the whole story. This is how it was in the Old Testament when men and women broke forth into praise as they witnessed the saving God at work. Such days have returned with the birth of Jesus.

What then should we notice especially about these verses? First, the way they combine personal and general – the very feature which causes the commentators so much trouble. They are a celebration both of the astonishing grace of God to Mary herself ('He has chosen even me!' verse 48) and of the wider dealings of God with the world. Is not genuine praise always of that double quality? Praise that never gets beyond the personal is inherently selfish; praise that never includes it is a sign that something is missing.

Secondly, they are an amazing leap of faith. 'He *has* put down the mighty from their seats . . .' There are plenty of people in the world who wish they were in a position to say that. This is a confident declaration of what will be — so confident that we can speak of it as though it had already happened. But then, Jesus has come, so the foundation has been laid, we know what the building will look like and can confidently speak of it as though it were finished.

Thirdly, God's positive discrimination. He disregards the power structures of the world and chooses an ordinary Jewish girl as the mother of the Lord (if we Protestants baulk at calling Mary 'blessed' (verse 48), we should at least remember that humanly speaking she was responsible for Jesus' earliest religious education). He unseats the tyrants and gives authority to the humble — not just as a form of tit-for-tat but because the world has hope of reaching its fulfilment only when it is ruled by the humble. The Magnificat is indeed a revolutionary document, but only in gentle hands.

Lastly, we come back to the promises (verses 54–55). To our way of thinking it may seem odd to place so much weight on particular Old Testament texts where God is said to promise future blessing to Abraham and his descendants. How can that be said to bind God for the future? But more is involved than mere words. The whole story unfolded in the Bible shows us a rescuing God who is both merciful and dependable. The coming of Jesus confirms it. The 'promises' are the witnesses to that consistency of God's character. If God cannot be trusted to be the same from day to day, religion may as well go out of business. But the witness of the Church through the centuries, and of Israel in the centuries before, is that God's mercy and saving power do not change. Jesus confirms it.

14

The Presentation of Jesus
Luke 2.21–40

WE are so accustomed to using verses 29–32 as a sort of spiritual night-cap at the end of a day that we may lose sight of their context and of the real thrust of what is being said in the passage as a whole.

The passage is part of a larger section in Luke, the overlapping stories of the births of John and Jesus which mark the beginning of a new era in God's dealings with the world. The two stories follow a similar pattern, annunciation, birth and, thirdly, a section in which the child is named and identified for what he is (Luke adds another episode about Jesus, without parallel in the story of John: his meeting with the professors in the temple). Both stories end with a note about the child growing up, ready for what is to come. Compare verses 39–40 with 1.80. In both stories the meaning is brought out in the hymns that are sung, by Mary, Zechariah, the angels and Simeon.

So this is a story of the presentation of Jesus in two senses: it is his presentation to God in the temple, not actually required by Old Testament law, but like the offering of Samuel by Hannah (I Sam 1.21–28) a consecration of the child by his parents to God. It is also the presentation of Jesus to the world (and to us as readers) as the one who fulfils all hopes and longings for a better world (verse 38).

What is striking is the emphasis on Jewish observance and the hopes of Israel. We are given a glimpse of ordinary Israelites, watching, waiting, praying and fasting for the day when God will redeem Israel. Herod is the local king, the Roman empire dominates the world and the people are far from free economically or politically – and that is only part of the picture. The later pages of the Gospel will tell of disease and mental disorder, of conflict and suffering, and a pervading sense of inadequacy and sin, private and corporate. Here are people confronting that situation with patient hope that one day God will turn things around and are prepared to pray and watch for its coming. There are such people today.

Everything in the passage sets Jewish piety in a good light and stresses that Jesus belongs to such people. He is circumcised as the law directs: so he becomes a Jew and subject to all the law of God requires. The sacrifices are offered – two turtledoves, the offering for a family of only modest means. It is Israel's hopes that are fulfilled by his coming – the gentiles are mentioned only once, in verses 31–32.

At a time when we can only be appalled at the continuing conflict in the Holy Land, when it is so difficult to feel sympathy with the policies of the state of Israel, both towards her neighbours and towards those whom the Bible calls 'the strangers within the gates', and when it is so easy in consequence to slide unawares into a kind of anti-semitism, it is important to remind ourselves that Jesus was a Jew and came to redeem Israel. In a sense the redemption of the rest of us is a by-product, though always part of God's long-term goal. The Jewish people have a special place in the purposes of God.

THE PRESENTATION OF JESUS

So the upshot of this passage is the good news that salvation has come. Both Simeon and Anna are described as prophets. Simeon is inspired by the Spirit like the prophets of the Old Testament. So what they say is not just personal intuition or wishful thinking; it is God-given insight. Although all that is visible to the naked eye is a small child, Simeon can now be discharged from his long vigil and go home to die in quiet confidence that all will be well.

But it is not all joy and peace. Verses 34–35 warn that the coming of Jesus will be a catastrophic event. Many will be brought down by it and some, who had no such expectations, will be uplifted. We are reminded of Mary's own words earlier (1.52), and of the Gospel story as it unfolds, good news for the poor, the despised and the penitent, and bad news for the rich, the arrogant and the complacent. The coming of salvation will be a painful time.

Mary herself will not escape the pain. The sword which will pierce her heart (verse 35) is probably not her grief at the death of Jesus (Luke does not depict her in such terms), but the challenge she herself will have to face, in the clash between the natural bonding of mother and son and the need to set that on one side if God's will is to be done (see 2.49–50, 8.19–21, 11.27–28).

And, of course, though it is only hinted at in the words 'spoken against' or 'opposed' in verse 34, there will be pain for Jesus himself. The salvation which Simeon has seen on the horizon can only come by means of the cross.

Nevertheless, Simeon can go to his rest in peace and we too can sleep more easily in our beds as a result. All those who watch and pray for deliverance can have courage to persevere. God's kingdom will come, and Jew and gentile will rejoice in it.

15
Mary and Martha
Luke 10.38–42

WHY was Martha in such a tizzy? If we could be sure of that we would have a better idea of the point of the story, though even with its uncertainties the point is clear enough.

Jesus and the disciples, at this point in Luke's Gospel, are on their way to Jerusalem and Martha's house is a stopover for the night. So an evening meal is essential. But Martha, in charge of the kitchen, is 'distracted about many things' and demands that her younger sister come and help. Why?

Unfortunately the earliest manuscripts of the Gospel offer different versions of Jesus' reply and they reflect different understandings of what Martha's problem was. The one that gets into the footnotes of most modern Bibles reads, 'You are anxious and bothered about many things, but few are needed, or just one.' On that interpretation, the problem was the menu. Martha had overdone it. Faced with the arrival of Jesus she wanted to put on an elaborate spread and then found she couldn't cope. Jesus points out that a simpler meal would have made the job easier and then she could have managed without her sister.

Plausible, but unlikely. For one thing, although it is

finely balanced, what Luke is most likely originally to have written is, 'You are anxious and bothered about many things, but only one is needed.' For another, it would not need an elaborate menu to cause Martha problems. Jesus, remember, is travelling with disciples (whether precisely 12 at this point hardly matters). The thought of even a straightforward meal for a dozen hungry young men arriving unannounced might drive even the most competent housekeeper spare. What Jesus is saying is far more dramatic. A meal is a good thing, but not a necessity. If it has to be a choice between eating and listening to the word of God, then the word wins every time.

That is the choice Mary, the younger sister, has made. She is 'seated at his feet listening to his word'. What that means is illustrated by Acts 22.3. Mary is on the floor, not for a shortage of chairs, nor because it is her favourite sitting posture, but because she is a disciple, along with the others, though not, as they are, a traveller. 'Sitting at the feet' was then (as, because of the Bible, it still is) a technical term for being a pupil. And Jesus defends that choice.

We let this element in the scene pass us by, often, without notice, but it is quite startling. For a woman to become the pupil of a rabbi was, at the time, quite unthinkable. That Jesus here not only permits it but actively defends her choice shows how radical was his approach to women. Mary is here on equal terms with Peter, James, John and the rest.

We don't know how the story ends. One of the chief characteristics of most stories about Jesus in the Gospels is that they finish with what Jesus says; that is why they are told in the first place and the narrative leads up to his pronouncement. Beyond that, there is no interest.

So we don't know whether Martha went back to the kitchen feeling thoroughly rebuked but still resentful, whether she took a more relaxed and less perfectionist attitude to the meal, whether she left the bread and meat to burn (like Alfred and the cakes) and sat down with her sister or whether Mary changed her mind and went to help her. Clearly the meal was needed, but Jesus has made the point: what really counts is listening to the word. The story shows no more interest in how Martha solved the practical problem posed by that than it does in telling us how to solve the practical consequences of Jesus' saying in our own lives.

It is not the only place the message crops up in Luke's writings. In Acts 6 the apostles refuse to be diverted from proclaiming the word of God by serving at tables. Others must be appointed to do that lesser task. And in Luke 21.34 disciples are warned against being distracted by the everyday concerns of the world so as to be caught unawares and unready in a time of crisis.

Perhaps most striking, however, is the fact that Luke chooses to put this story in chapter 10 immediately following the parable which, perhaps more than any other passage, emphasises practical service to others as the way to eternal life, the story of the good Samaritan, with its marching orders 'go and do likewise'. Immediately Luke corrects the balance. One thing is really necessary: hearing Jesus' word. That word includes 'go and do likewise' but also embraces very much more. And unless, like Mary, we first become a disciple, we shall not be equipped for the practical serving. Is that why we so easily become distracted in our efforts?

One last comment: we so easily read these stories with modern blinkers on. We do not notice, for example, how unusual it would be for Mary to join the disciples. I deliberately referred to them just now as young men, for that is the impression the New Testament gives. How old was Martha, or her younger sister? We have no means of knowing. My (quite arbitrary) guess is that Mary was about 15.

16
Prayer
Luke 11.1–13

THERE is far more in this short passage on prayer than can be dealt with in these brief notes. Indeed, nothing can do justice to the Lord's prayer. One of its remarkable features is that the closer we examine what it says, the less we understand its precise meaning. The exact meaning of the Greek behind 'daily bread', for example, has been obscure even to Greek speakers since at least AD 200. Yet in the end it does not matter, because words of prayer are never just like fossils to be examined but rather like jump-leads to get our own prayers going.

The passage offers us three reasons for praying. The first is, Jesus prayed. Luke especially shows Jesus as 'our praying pattern' (to use Charles Wesley's phrase). That is what impels the disciples to ask him in verse 1 to teach them. If prayer was important for him, it can hardly be less so for us. If we ask why that should be, the first word of the prayer gives the answer: 'Father'.

Luke's version of the prayer is shorter than the one in Matthew 6 and generally regarded as closer to the original Jesus taught. Compare it in a modern English translation with Matthew's version and you will soon see how much simpler and more direct it is, and nothing more so than the one word 'Father', unparalleled in its directness in Jewish prayers ancient or modern. It brings God's relationship with us out of the generality of God-with-Israel or God-with-the-human-race ('our Father') into the sharp focus of God-with-me. That is how it was for Jesus. That is what disciples are invited to discover by using this prayer.

A second reason for prayer is given in verses 5 to 13. The key to them is in verse 13 – 'how much more'. If even a sleepy householder can be roused to help a friend, for the sake of peace and quiet if not for friendship, how much more can God, who is neither sleepy nor reluctant, be relied on to answer a call for help! If normal human parents, who have no pretensions to moral perfection ('being evil', verse 13), can be relied on to respond to their children's needs and not play cruel jokes on them, how much more God, the holy one!

When I am reading these verses aloud, I am never sure where to put the emphasis: '*Ask* and it will be given you' or 'Ask and it will be *given* you'? Is the emphasis on the householder's willingness to get up and lend bread or on the persistence of the man at the door who won't take no for an answer? In the end it is both. It is because God is willing to give that we are encouraged to ask and go on asking. God gives in response to our asking.

Of course, it is not always quite like that. Prayer, it seems, is not always answered and persistence does not always pay off. But we must not be too pedantic about this passage. These words of Jesus are a form of encouragement, not a guarantee. 'Come to sunny Blackpool' is an encouragement to visitors to make the trip and, judging by the numbers who go back each year, they do not feel let down. But no one ever imagines it never rains on the Lancashire coast. A Meteorological Office survey would show the precise number of days of rain and shine, but no tourist board would simply quote it. Encouragement highlights the good things, urges people to take the chance, to act in faith, for there is indeed sunshine to be had. But it is not a guarantee of no rain.

But there is another point, which takes us back to the Lord's prayer. Look at it again in all its starkness. One sentence ('Give us our bread') relates directly to our needs. The rest focuses on God. His name is to be shown to be holy and recognised as such by all. His kingdom is to come. We ask for forgiveness because only so can we serve him. We commit ourselves to forgiving others because that is his will. So too we ask to be preserved from temptation, those tests under which our loyalty might crack, so that we may remain faithful to God. These are not the requests of those who use prayer for their own ends. But then, that is not what prayer is for. Perhaps to emphasise the point Luke ends verse 13 by referring to the Holy Spirit, the greatest of God's good gifts (contrast Matt 7.11).

I said there were three reasons for praying in this passage. The Lord's prayer itself is the third. It is a badge of discipleship, marking out Jesus' disciples from John's (verse 1). This is not how everyone prays, but it is how we pray if we are truly his disciples. We pray as he did, sharing his access to the Father. We commit ourselves to seeing the world through his eyes, as the scene where God's holiness is to be demonstrated and his kingdom to come. We commit ourselves to living as he did, forgiving others, trusting in God, not failing the test. It is not enough just to repeat the Lord's prayer. We have to make it our own.

17
The Rich Fool
Luke 12.13–21

WHAT would you have done in the farmer's shoes? Where did he go wrong? We are so used to calling him 'the rich fool' that we might not stop to think what options he had and where his folly really lay.

He had a windfall. There is an element of uncertainty even in modern farming, although science can help cushion the effects of uncertain weather. But among Jesus' contemporaries drought, crop disease and pests were a real threat and a bumper harvest something to celebrate. The farmer did not achieve it through hard slog (though he must have worked hard); it came out of the blue. He must have felt like the modern winner of the lottery jackpot. But unlike his modern counterpart he will have seen it as a gift of God, from whom every good harvest came.

So he stockpiled it. He couldn't guarantee another bumper crop. Next year there might be famine. And if he thought about his Bible, there was the example of Joseph in Egypt, storing up seven years' good harvests so as to survive seven years' bad ones (Genesis 41.46–57). What was wrong in that? Any one who has taken out life insurance or a personal pension plan might ask the same question. We have to provide for the future.

The trouble was, he never lived to enjoy it. Sudden death can always strike. So there was the absurdity of full barns and no one to enjoy them. But what about his family, wife, children, other relatives? They could benefit. We might well ask, for there is no mention of them, and perhaps that is symptomatic. He is unlikely to have been a bachelor – few were – but other people do not seem to have entered his thought.

Which leads us to verse 21, the climax and the key to the parable. There are two crucial phrases in it, 'for themselves' and 'not rich towards God'. Wealth as such is not the issue but what we do with it and where it is banked.

In order to go further into this we need to move on to another parable, in Luke 16.19–31, about another rich man, who also lived it up on his wealth (compare 16.19 with 12.19). He too comes to grief when death strikes and his wealth has gone. What can stand him in good stead then? The answer is plain: there was a poor man he was too selfish to help, not at a distance where he might have pleaded ignorance, but right on his doorstep. If he had shared his prosperity with Lazarus, things would have been different when the day of reckoning came.

So with the farmer in chapter 12. Getting rich suddenly was not a sin. Thinking only of himself and how he could enjoy it was. He was a fool, in the profound and disturbing biblical sense of that word, in that he paid no attention to those things which would affect his eternal destiny. What would he be able to say to his maker, when the question our maker always asks is not about us but about our brothers and sisters? To have no answer to give to that is poverty indeed.

So now we see why this parable of the farmer follows

on from verses 13 to 15. In Jewish law the normal way to divide an inheritance (of which the key part would be land) was in the proportion of two to one in favour of the elder son. In this case either the two brothers could not agree on the sums, or there were other legal complications, or one brother wanted to keep the estate intact as a more economic working unit while the other wanted to strike out on his own, perhaps sell up and take the proceeds.

Jesus refuses to be an arbitrator. He is not a lawyer qualified for such work. But there is a deeper issue. What has made this dispute so acrimonious that they have to turn to arbitration is that both want as much as they can get and neither will let go. Neither, apparently, has heard of generosity.

It all boils down to the same thing. We cannot survive for long in this world without material goods, food, clothing and shelter at least. Human dignity and even a modest degree of self-fulfilment call for rather more than that. The uncertainties of life make it reasonable to provide for the future: indeed, to neglect to do so when we are able to would be irresponsible. It is another form of selfishness simply to assume that someone else will look after us. So we need to earn and save. Yet all that can become a distraction that destroys the soul, binding us ever more tightly in a web of self-absorption, like a spider binding up a fly, until we are incapable of reaching out to anyone beyond ourselves. The Bible has a simple word for it, greed. It will leave us speechless before God.

18

The Road to Emmaus
Luke 24.13–35

WHY does Luke tell this story here? Because he believed it happened so? Surely, but things are rarely so simple in the Gospels. In fact, if we look through the whole of this chapter we can see Luke not only rounding off the crucifixion with the resurrection but doing two other things besides. He is pointing out the meaning of the entire story the Gospel has told from chapter one onwards, and he is underlining the missionary commission: disciples must go and tell. This episode fits into that scheme.

The key is in verse 16. The two travellers are prevented from recognising Jesus. It is no accident that they don't notice who he is; it is not just that they are too preoccupied to look him in the eye. They are not allowed to recognise him, not yet.

That makes them like us. The consistent New Testament emphasis is that the visual appearances of Jesus happened for a time but then stopped. They are not granted to us. Like the two on the road, we have to make do with other people's testimony that Jesus has risen from the dead. Like them, we don't quite know what to make of it. Did it really happen? What precisely happened? How could it have happened? Like them, we have to rely on the testimony of the women and (because, unlike them, we have the rest of the New Testament before us) the testimony of other disciples and of Paul. But, like the two on the road, we can't see for ourselves. We have to believe the testimony – or not. No experiment could be invented which would give us 'proof'.

But that is not their only problem – or ours. They are struggling with an age-old conundrum, still presenting itself today. They had set their hopes on Jesus, thought God's kingdom would come, and had seen him crushed. Religious men, cynical men and brutal men had made conspiracy. A wicked world had reasserted itself. How can one believe in God in such a world? So news of a resurrection is not only bewildering; if it is not true, it is a mockery.

Just our problems. So these two (men? man and wife? man and boy?) on the Emmaus Road are our representatives, facing our problems. So what Jesus says to them he says through them to us. That is why Luke tells the story. And what does Jesus say? Believe! There is no other remedy. But why believe? Because that is what the Scriptures say (verses 25–27).

The appeal to prophecy is not a business of finding proof-texts. In fact it is very difficult to find explicit texts in the Old Testament foretelling the death and resurrection of the Messiah. But the pattern of death and resurrection is there throughout: Abraham, sacrificing Isaac and getting him back again, Joseph, preserved to become the benefactor of his destroyers, Elijah, despairing of life and given hope, Israel, taken into exile and brought back again. Death and resurrection, losing one's life and gaining it, being lost and being found, are God's pattern all through the Bible, as they are in creation itself – 'unless a seed dies, it abides alone, but if it dies it bears much fruit'

(John 12.24). So the story of Jesus dying and rising is credible – it fits God's pattern. Far from casting doubt on Jesus' credentials as the redeemer who brings God's kingdom, it endorses them.

That is the lesson for the two travellers and for us. It should be enough. The rest is faith. Yet, as an act of grace, something they did not need and should have done without, they are granted something more. Their eyes are opened and they see Jesus for themselves. At this point they part company from us. They are not in our shoes struggling with the Easter story. They become witnesses to us of what it means.

But still Luke tells his story carefully, full of clues for us to pick up. We may not see Jesus as they did, for such appearances do not repeat themselves, but we can know his presence 'in the breaking of bread', that act which recalls the Last Supper and all Jesus' meals with his friends and points us forward to the kingdom feast yet to come. Like them, we may become aware of his presence, not when we choose, for we cannot conjure up that presence at will, but as a gift, a moment of revelation, given when God wills. Like them, we shall have the presence of Jesus 'on the way' (for Luke all discipleship is a journey with Jesus), even though we do not know he is there.

But let us be clear what that presence, recognised or unrecognised, implies. It is not a mere feeling of 'someone there'. It is the presence of an interpreter, who helps us to see disaster and hope as God's pattern of working in the world. It is the presence of one who died and rose and gives himself to us to revive and sustain us. The two disciples had hoped he would be the redeemer who brings God's kingdom. On the road and at the table they discover that he is.

19

The Word
John 1.1–18

NOBODY can expect to do justice to this passage, and certainly not in 800 words. Part of the challenge is that we do not know precisely what weight the words carry. Words can ring different bells for different people and we do not know enough about the first readers of the Gospel to be sure how the passage would strike them. They have been variously identified as intellectual pagans, cosmopolitan Jews, Christians with a Jewish (or, to the contrary, a pagan) background and so on.

But more profoundly the difficulty is that here we are on the edge of mystery. Who was Jesus? How is he related to God? We can grope for understanding and the words to express it, but, God being God, we shall never get to the bottom of it.

So all I offer you here is a few entry points into the passage. If you want to get deeper you will have to turn to the big books.

First, notice its cutting edge. There are some negative things being said. There were clearly some people around who held John the Baptist in high honour (did they think of him as the light?). Verse 8 cuts him down to size. There were those who believed that the wisdom by which God created the universe, the wisdom that enlightens all wise people the world over, was embodied in the law of Moses (if your Bible includes the Apocrypha, look at Ecclesiasticus 24). For John's Gospel the law is indeed given by Moses (verse 17) but the divine word that spoke the world into existence and enlightens every human being is to be found, not there, but in Jesus the Son of God. In him God's nature, his grace and truth, is to be found. No nonsense here about all religions being the same in the end. But equally no nonsense either about truth being found in Jesus and nowhere else. He is the light that has shone from the beginning. He is the embodiment, and the judge, of all true insight. He both affirms and judges all faiths.

Secondly, notice how the passage brings together creation and salvation. The word spoken from the beginning becomes flesh. The Christian who thinks that the doctrine of creation is just an optional extra, something for the textbooks, while the real business of Christianity is about believing in Jesus and getting saved, has missed the point. Jesus is not worth believing in, and certainly cannot deliver salvation, unless he embodies all that is fundamental about life. If in the real world there are other forces at work, other truths we might shipwreck on, he is no saviour. This passage binds creation and salvation, because only the creator can save.

Then notice how many characteristic words and ideas from John's Gospel crop up in this passage. Three examples will do. *Witness*: John the Baptist is a witness to Jesus – indeed that is his only function (verse 23). The notion of witnesses is very important to John. We do not see God's truth on our own. Others point us to it, who have seen it first. The fact that there are so many, pointing from different angles, is partly what assures us we are on the right track. In that sense the Gospel itself is a witness. 'We beheld his glory' (verse 14) – 'These things are written that you may believe' (20.31).

Another key word is *believe* (verse 12). There is nothing open-and-shut about Jesus. He does not wear a placard saying 'I am the Son of God' (would it make any difference if he did?). We have to see the clues, face the challenge, make up our minds. The rewards are great – we enter the company of God's children – but it is not easy, and not every one gets there.

That leads on to the third theme, *rejection*. As early as verse 10 we are warned how the Gospel story will unfold. Jesus will come as the great divider, separating those who rise to the challenge and believe and those who don't. But those who don't do not remain neutral. They become the resistance, part of the forces that in the end send him to the cross and afterwards hate and persecute his followers (15.18). There are no neutrals in this Gospel. Everything is light or darkness, truth or falsehood, even if to our eyes things seem more ambiguous and blurred.

So John's Gospel shows us Jesus as the one who joins creation and salvation, eternity and time, the one who is God's bodily presence in the world he has himself made; a hidden presence, for people have to make up their minds about him; a presence powerful yet vulnerable, never more in command than when he is handed over to be crucified.

I suppose in our simple way we tend to think that this means that Jesus is a sort of messenger from heavenly space, one sent from God to us, bound as we are in space and time. At one level that is true, and there are texts in John's Gospel to support it. Jesus is the archetypal missionary (20.21). But there is a deeper truth in verse 18. There is a sense in which Jesus never leaves the Father whom he represents. He remains in close communion, 'in the bosom of the Father' (cf 8.29). He does not so much come from heaven to earth as join the two together.

20
The Wedding at Cana
John 2.1–11

IT is easy to get distracted in reading this passage and lose our way. Travel too far down the road of asking 'What really happened?' and we might end up with a reconstruction of events that does Jesus no credit, turning him into a wonder-worker who produces a bit of wizardry just to help a friend out of a jam – and on a grotesque scale, for 150 gallons of wine is a lot for any wedding. That is not the impression John wants to give.

On the other hand, John is fond of dropping hints. The Gospel is full of them, inviting us all the time to see deeper meaning in what we read. The problem then is, we might find hints where none might be intended. All sorts of plausible things can be read into this narrative, many of them harmless enough, but a distraction from the central theme.

We have to start from John's summing-up in verse 11. What happened was a sign, it revealed Jesus' glory and it led to faith. 'Sign' is one of John's favourite words. He uses it of an event which reveals who Jesus is and what he does, a pointer to the truth about him which is so deep it is better expressed, and more movingly, in symbols than in plain prose. I say 'movingly' because when we grasp that truth it moves us to believe. For what we glimpse in a sign is the glory of the creator God shining in Jesus his one and only Son. A real glimpse of that makes us throw all we have and are into the ring with him. What happened in Cana was such a sign. The disciples believed.

So what produced that effect? Verse 10 suggests the answer. It is the climax of the story and in all Gospel stories it is the climax that counts. 'You have kept the best wine till last.' So what is important is not how the wine was made (the speaker does not know about that, verse 9) but its quality; it is better than anything before. So Jesus, John is saying, and what he brings, is better than anything before. God has kept the really good thing until now.

But this good thing does not come out of the blue. The wine is made out of the water set aside for purification according to Old Testament law and Jewish custom. Often it is said the story teaches that Jesus supersedes Jewish religion, replacing water by wine. It is more accurate to say that he converts the one into the other. The value of the old is not denied, but it is enhanced and brought to fulfilment when Jesus comes.

Then there is the puzzling dialogue between Jesus and his mother at the beginning. Jesus sounds abrupt and even rude to us, because we wrap our conversation up in words like 'please' that many other cultures do not bother with. But Jesus does make a response here that comes elsewhere in John. God has sent him, and only God gives the orders. His life throughout is an expression of total obedience to the Father. So if Jesus is to act, it is not because any human being thinks it is a good idea, but because the Father directs.

And part of the problem is the timing. The place where God's glory will be truly revealed, and all will be able to see who Jesus is and what he does, will be the cross (see 12.23, 13.31). Only then will disciples come to the full depths of faith. The time for that has not yet come. So what Jesus does now can only foreshadow it, sketch out in symbol what one day will be seen. But that reminder of what is to come underlines the cost of this new wine. The life it symbolises is available to us only at the cost of his life.

So what did happen? We are left with that question unanswered. John is not very interested. He passes over it, saying no more, in effect, than one minute there was water, the next there was wine – but what superb wine!

I originally chose this passage for January because it has been used in lectionaries from very early times at Epiphany, January 6, because that was the date of the festival of Dionysus, the god also credited with turning water into wine. So, the early Church declared, all that earlier religion sought after and recognised in God was fulfilled in Jesus. Through him pagan water was turned into Christian wine.

So what for us today? Many Christian converts witness to the new wine of the Gospel. Some are particularly conscious of the break between the old and the new in their lives. Perhaps on reflection they might come to see it was truly a conversion, a change, for the past held insights and experiences which were also of God, but were transformed, at long last, into life-giving wine by Jesus. Others cannot look back to such a landmark in their lives. But we are all invited to see the glory of God in Jesus and receive by faith the new life, which nothing on earth can touch for comparison.

21

The Woman Taken in Adultery
John 7.53–8.11

YOU might have difficulty in finding this passage. In many modern Bibles it is relegated to the foot of the page or to the end of John's Gospel. It does not appear in the earliest manuscripts and is certainly not part of the original text. But there is a strong case for regarding it as an early story about Jesus which circulated by word of mouth and eventually got included in John, and certainly the Church for centuries has regarded it as part of canonical Scripture. It is worth looking at.

Adultery in Jewish law of the time could only occur if the woman involved was married. There were no general prescriptions against a married man resorting to other women. If convicted of adultery, both the man and woman were to be executed by stoning. For such a conviction a minimum of two witnesses was required and after sentence had been passed they had to cast the first stones (a rough and ready deterrent against bringing accusations lightly).

They bring the woman to Jesus, not to act as judge, but to put him on the spot (verse 6). It is unlikely that the formal court hearing has taken place. Possibly they are on their way to court or even intend to deal with her by lynch law without formal hearing.

What they are after is a statement from Jesus that they can use against him. There is evidence that under Roman rule at this time the Jewish courts had been deprived of the power to pass a death sentence (John 18.31). So if Jesus says she is to be stoned, he is in trouble with the Romans, if he says she is not to be, he is convicted of contradicting God's law as given to Moses.

So they are using this woman to get at Jesus. It matters nothing to them that the humiliation she has already experienced should be added to by this public exposure. But there are yet more unsavoury elements to this tale.

She was caught in the act, not just by one person but by several. One person making a chance discovery is possible, but a whole group coming upon the scene suggests a tip-off; by her husband? And where is the man involved? Commentaries suggest he escaped. With so many people bursting in on the scene one has to suspect they deliberately let him get away. And why are they so indignant about what they have found? Are they really concerned about the broken marriage of a friend or simply zealous that the law should be kept and the woman be made a public example?

Jesus 'wrote on the ground'. It is useless to speculate what he wrote; if it had been important the story would have mentioned it. The word can also mean to draw. Jesus buys time by doodling, avoiding giving the incriminating answer they are seeking and building up pressure on them by suspense, until he throws the challenge back to them: 'Let the innocent cast the first stone' – innocent not just of adultery but of all the sordid motives behind their actions in this case. They fade away and the woman is left confronting Jesus.

'Neither do I condemn you (that is, condemn you to death); go and sin no more.' It is a harder saying than we sometimes think. Where can she go (in the society of the time) but back to her husband? It was possibly the tension between a loveless arranged marriage and an affair of the heart that had led to the adultery. Possibly her husband had tipped off his friends and would have been glad to be rid of her. He will hold it against her for ever after. Perhaps he will divorce her and return her to her father. Who will marry her then? Everyone in the village will remember her for it until her dying day. But at least she has her life, and the chance of a new beginning, and the memory of one man who treated her with dignity, integrity and compassion and so gave her an insight into the loving mercy of God.

It is not easy to draw parallels between this story and our modern situation. Most marriages today are built on very different assumptions. But now, as then, adultery involves a betrayal of trust that strikes at the root of the securities upon which family life, for adults and children, is based. There is nothing in Jesus' words to condone it. He treats it as a sin.

But we delude ourselves if we think that is where the story chiefly bites. It exposes, as in a mirror, the mixed and degrading motives from which we sometimes pursue righteous causes, the callous way we use other people to serve our ends and the fanaticism that can overtake us when principles become more important than the people they are supposed to enhance. It reminds us of the double standards which so often victimise women.

It also reminds us that there is no easy road to repentance and that being forgiven does not mean

THE WOMAN TAKEN IN ADULTERY   83

that everything suddenly becomes magically easy. But it does set before us the picture of Jesus, who deals with us as human beings with specific needs and not as mere cases in an ideological argument about how to uphold standards. In him we can see the face of God.

22

Jesus and the Spirit
John 14.15–26

WE are fascinated by John's Gospel as by the waters of a deep and silent pool. But it is difficult to fathom. The words are very simple and there are no long complicated sentences such as we find in Paul. Yet the meaning often escapes us.

John's language is not the prose of the journalist but the imagery of the poet. He does not spoon-feed us with ideas; he pushes us to go exploring for ourselves, believing that the Holy Spirit will take the words of Jesus and unveil their depth.

One example of what I mean is the way parts of this passage have more than one layer of meaning. Remember the setting: Jesus and his disciples are at supper before his arrest. We are looking forward to the events that will follow. Jesus will be taken away from the disciples and after three days come back to them. Only the inner circle of disciples and friends will see him, not Pilate nor Caiaphas nor the crowds. Then he will depart from them again, and they will look for his return in glory. In his place the Holy Spirit will come. It all seems to be touched on in verses 16, 18–19, 22.

Yet when we look more closely it is not the outward visible return of Jesus which is in mind but something more inward, less tied to time. Verses 21 and 23 describe a coming of Jesus, not as a public event, nor to the eleven at Easter, but to any believer who loves him and keeps his commandments. So the 'seeing' which the disciples enjoy but is denied to the world is not the sight of the eyes but the discernment that comes with faith and love.

But if Jesus comes, so does the Spirit (verse 16), the Spirit who brings truth, the Holy Spirit who interprets Jesus for those who come after (verse 26). There is a lot of discussion about what the words 'counsellor', 'comforter' or 'paraclete' mean. The most important word in verse 16 however is 'another'; Jesus is the first. Whatever Jesus has been to the disciples in the past, the Spirit will be in the future. They will not be left alone like orphans.

Those who like their doctrine of the Trinity nice and tidy, with separate jobs for each of the Persons to do, will be baffled by this passage. It speaks equally of Jesus, or of Jesus and the Father together, coming to us and also of Jesus sending the Spirit. The truth, looked at one way, is that the human bodily presence of Jesus has been succeeded by the unseen presence of the Spirit; but from a different viewpoint we can see that, just as God the Father was encountered in the person of Jesus, so Jesus, and therefore the Father, is encountered in the person of the Spirit.

So the seeds of the later doctrine of the Trinity are to be found in this passage. But remember that the Trinity was the experience of the Church in worship and discipleship long before it was a doctrine. Trinity Sunday is not a day to dread when sermons have to be wrapped up in obscurity, but a day for celebrating our experience of the wonderful mystery of God in his dealings with us.

So the thrust of this little passage is pretty clear. We are not left to fend for ourselves like orphans. Easter and Pentecost mean the living presence of the risen Jesus in the Spirit with his Church: more than that, with every believer, in an intimate inner conversation.

Thirty years ago it was fashionable to ask what was the 'cash value' of such statements. If they sound mysterious, is that because we are on the edge of a genuine mystery or because we are deceiving ourselves with fine-sounding words which don't actually mean anything?

This is where verse 17 comes in, repeating a point often made in this Gospel and elsewhere in the New Testament. Unless you have been in touch with God – better, unless God has touched you – the language of faith will not make much sense. It is like falling in love. Romantic language may be dismissed as sentimental rubbish, until experience makes it come alive. So the awkward question, always, about John's Gospel is, 'Is this truly obscure, or am I lacking the clue?'

There is, however, one recurring theme in this passage which keeps it earthed: 'If you love me, you will keep my commandments' (verses 15, 21, 23, 24). This is no airy-fairy spirituality which revels in secret communion with God, unknown to those outside and making no earthly difference to anybody. It has to pass a stern test: does it spring out of, and result in, the tough practical love of Jesus that is expressed in obedience – supremely, obedience to the 'new commandment' (13.34) to love one another. Any claimed spirituality which is not marked by this, however impressive the talk and however profound the experience, is phoney.

23
The Vine
John 15.1–17

ONE of the frustrating things about John's Gospel for people with tidy minds is that you can never be quite sure what any passage means. As soon as you think you've got the meaning pinned down, the next sentence introduces fresh dimensions. Almost every word seems to bring with it a crowd of meanings, echoes, associations, all demanding to be given weight. So don't expect me to go through verse by verse and deliver a cut and dried interpretation. Rather, I will try to pick out a few faces in the crowd.

It begins with 'I am'. In a number of places in this Gospel Jesus lays claim to great Old Testament ideas and shows himself to be their fulfilment (eg 6.48, 8.12, 10.7, 11). What people have long looked for in their religious life, and to some extent have found, is here available in its true form and fullness.

In this passage Jesus is the vine. In the Old Testament, Israel, as God's people, were a vine or vineyard planted and tended by God, with often disappointing, even disastrous, results (Psalm 80.8–18, Isa 5.1–7). Here Jesus with his disciples form the community where God's hopes and promises may be fulfilled – Jesus with his disciples, for the whole point of the passage is the relationship between disciples and the Lord. It is not Jesus alone who is the vine, but Jesus with the disciples.

So, like Paul's great image of the Church as the body of Christ, this passage lays emphasis on the togetherness of discipleship. They are to love one another (verse 12). Jesus speaks to his hearers as a group; every 'you' is a genuine plural. As John Wesley was to say much later, there is no such thing as solitary Christianity.

Yet the main stress nevertheless is on the relation of each individual to the Lord from whom alone we can draw life. Each is to be 'in him' and he in each. Branches only live if they draw life from the tree of which they are part.

This indwelling seems at times to be an inward, spiritual affair, a matter of faith, prayer and love. Yet Christ abiding in us is used interchangeably with his teaching abiding in us. There is a moral dimension; not only prayer but obedience.

And things must stay that way. A key word here, as elsewhere in John's Gospel, is 'abide' or 'remain'. It describes the permanence of the loving communion between Father and Son (verse 10). That must be true also of the disciple with the Lord.

So thoughts about discipleship tumble over each other, each drawing out something of what it means: drawing on Christ for life; obedience to his commands (verse 10); absorbing his teaching and understanding it (verse 15) so that it becomes part of us and directs our behaviour from within (verses 3,7); loving him and giving ourselves totally in love to one another, which means his love is active within us (verses 9,12,13); and on top of all that, constancy and consistency, staying the course in a relationship of that quality, when, as we know, life is never such a steady stream, but includes many ups and downs and we blow hot and cold.

There is a sharp edge to this passage – pruning-knife sharp. I am told (not being a gardener myself) that there are two stages in pruning a vine. The first is ruthlessly cutting out the dead wood, the second – later – is picking off some of the buds to enable the rest to thrive. The message is clear: not only that those who cease drawing life from Christ lose their partnership in the people of God (an observable fact, often; they simply 'drop off' as we say), but that there can be no fruitful continuing without cost and pain. Something has to go (frequently) if we are to stay fruitful.

And what is this fruit? There is no single answer. The emphasis moves from obedience (verse 7) to love (verse 12) to going out to make disciples (verse 16). And surely none of these is possible without the other. Abiding in Christ is not a cosy comfort session for the self-centred; it is vigorous, outward-looking and missionary. That is the test of whether we have got the real thing.

But the rigour and persistence demanded of us is more than matched by what is on offer. Here we are drawn into the life of God and into his outward movement of love to the world, whose eternal Son laid down his life for his friends (verse 13). Here is the true vine in whom all human hopes and needs find fulfilment.

John does not mention the institution of the Sacrament of Holy Communion in this chapter (though he surely knows of it, 6.53). But it is difficult to think of belonging to Christ the true vine without thinking also of the cup of wine that was his blood. Not that the Eucharist is for John the only vehicle by which that relationship is sustained (he perhaps omits any reference to underline the fact that it is not), but 'abiding in the vine' is at the centre of what the Eucharist expresses and conveys. At all events it was a wise choice when in 1928 or thereabouts it became customary in Methodism to use the first eight verses of this passage in the Covenant service. How better to call attention to the only terms on which real discipleship is possible?

24
Thomas
John 20.24–31

YOU can't read the story of Thomas without including verses 30–31, for they are the climax of the story. In fact they are the climax of the whole Gospel, so much so that many scholars believe chapter 21 was added later, by the original author or someone else.

Thomas is offered all that subsequent generations of Christians have had to make do with, the joyful testimony of those who had seen the risen Jesus. Not with them when Jesus originally came, Thomas is invited to share their faith none the less. But he finds it too much; he demands tangible proof – more indeed than they had been given, for they had been content with just seeing.

So a week later Thomas is offered what he asked for, but discovers he does not need it. Sight is enough and he makes his great confession of faith. Even so, he gets more than you and I are given. We have to depend on the word of those who first saw.

It is the temper of our age to demand proof of everything. If we are told someone has been seen trying to break in at the back window, we go to check whether there are signs that a person was there. If we do find marks, we want to check they weren't made by the cat. Similarly, when we are told the first disciples saw the risen Jesus, we want proof they were not hallucinating. Was the tomb empty? But even that is not conclusive proof; it might have been a different tomb or the body might have been stolen. And so on, all equivalent to 'If I cannot touch the scars, I will not believe.' This passage drives home, through the story of Thomas, the painful truth, we have to believe. We are not given 'hard' evidence to provide 'proof'.

So the Gospel was written to help its readers believe. There is a clear link between verses 29 and 31. Verses 30–31 are an explicit statement of what is really the purpose of all four Gospels. They were not written as historical records for future scholars to study. Nor were they written as memoirs by doddering old disciples who feared that their memory was letting them down. They were written to share faith. They were written out of a burning desire that the faith which had taken possession of the first believers, and the life which they knew they experienced in consequence, might be shared by others. They were an instrument of the mission of the Church – Gospels, 'good newses'.

That is why the Gospels reach across the centuries to us. They bring to us the joyful testimony of the first believers and their invitation to us to share their faith. (I use the word 'joyful' because it is the key to the whole chapter and especially verses 19–23, with its contrast between fear and joy; see also 16.20)

But what we are invited to believe is not just that, miraculously, Jesus rose from the dead. Thomas' confession in verse 28 is the high-point in New Testament statements about Jesus. He is Lord and God. In him we come face to face with our creator and deliverer. From him we can receive life that transcends the limits of the seventy-plus years we may hope to exist on earth, both in quality and in duration.

That, in the setting this Gospel gives it, is a profound reassurance. The disciples are gathered together in a closed room for fear of what may happen to them (verses 19, 26). They feel powerless and under threat. They are a tiny minority in a big city. The only protection they can find is in each other's company. It is a far cry from the commission they have received, 'As the Father has sent me, so I send you' (verse 21). Without the presence of Jesus, the Lord and God, they, and all little groups of believers after them, will remain huddled away in secrecy and fear. Fortified by that knowledge, however, though they will still be few and vulnerable, they will become witnesses through whom others will believe (cf 17.20).

But notice two other points: first, the one who comes face to face with us as Lord and God carries the scars of crucifixion in his hands and side. There is no divorce between Good Friday and Easter; they are inseparable. We are invited to believe in a crucified Lord, and that is the faith that leads to life. Secondly, Thomas' faith is personal, my Lord and God, with all the implications of personal commitment, obedience, engagement of mind and heart that the little word 'my' carries.

So the main question this passage leaves with us is, what do we read the Gospels for? Is it for historical interest, the study of ancient language and literature, or, as with poetry, appreciation of good writing (none of them bad motives so far as they go)? Or to catch a personal faith?

But of course most of those who first encountered this Gospel (and most people centuries after) could not read. If you were an ordinary first-century Christian you did not read the Gospels, you heard them. Someone read them aloud in the weekly gathering for worship. There is a hint of that in verse 26. It was eight days later (ie, by ancient ways of counting, one week) that the disciples gathered again, this time with Thomas. So Jesus is felt to be present (but no longer seen), Sunday by Sunday, and still the challenge is given: believe the witnesses, acknowledge him as your Lord and God and receive life.